Dear Reader,

It is with great humility and a sense of purpose that I present to you this book, "Global Boiling: Confronting the Crisis of Our Time." As the author, my name is Marco A. S. Y., and my journey in crafting this literary exploration of the climate crisis has been one of profound discovery, urgency, and hope.

The inspiration for this book emerged from a deep concern for the future of our planet and a profound realization of the dire consequences of global warming. Witnessing the alarming rise in temperatures, the intensification of extreme weather events, and the growing impacts on ecosystems and communities, I knew that I could not remain idle. The time to act is now, and the imperative to raise awareness and foster collective action is a responsibility I could not ignore.

Through extensive research and contemplation, I endeavored to present a comprehensive understanding of global boiling—the sobering reality that the era of global warming has ended, and we now face the era of global boiling. It is my hope that these pages provide you with the knowledge and insights needed to comprehend the severity of the climate crisis while also illuminating the potential pathways to a sustainable and just future.

Throughout this journey, I have encountered stories of hope and resilience amidst adversity. The actions of individuals, communities, and movements working tirelessly to address climate change have fueled my optimism for a better world. In these pages, I seek to amplify those voices, inspire collective action, and foster a sense of responsibility to protect the Earth for current and future generations.

This book is not solely a portrayal of a crisis; it is **a call to action**. We are all interconnected on this precious planet, and the impacts of global boiling touch each and every one of us. The journey towards sustainability requires a unified effort, transcending borders and ideologies. It necessitates embracing climate justice, recognizing our shared responsibility, and cherishing the sanctity of nature.

I invite you to delve into the chapters that explore the causes and consequences of global boiling, the role of innovation and technology, and the significance of collective action. Together, let us engage in honest reflection, elevate our understanding, and summon the courage to confront the challenges that lie ahead.

In closing, I extend my heartfelt gratitude to you, dear reader, for joining me on this transformative exploration. It is my sincerest hope that this book inspires you to become an agent of change, to champion sustainability in all aspects of life, and to contribute to the restoration and preservation of our beloved planet.

May the stories within these pages kindle the flames of hope in your heart and propel us all towards a sustainable future.

With utmost sincerity,

Marco A. S. Y.

Chapters

Introduction:

In this opening chapter, we set the stage for the profound shift that has taken place in our climate, propelling us into a new era known as "global boiling." We delve into the origins of this term and its implications for the future of our planet. As we explore the alarming evidence and declarations made by experts, the urgency of addressing this crisis becomes abundantly clear.

Chapter 1: The Arrival of Global Boiling

Section 1: Farewell to Global Warming

We begin by reflecting on the previous era of "global warming" and how it has led us to this pivotal moment. We examine the historical context of climate change, including the scientific discoveries that initially sparked concerns about rising temperatures and their consequences.

Section 2: The UN Chief's Stark Warning

In this section, we delve into the profound impact of the United Nations Chief's recent warning that global warming is no longer sufficient to describe the severity of our situation. We explore the reasons behind the shift in terminology to "global boiling" and the weight of responsibility this places on humanity to take immediate action.

Section 3: July: Earth's Hottest Month on Record

The evidence of "global boiling" becomes starkly evident as we analyze the data confirming July as the hottest month ever recorded on Earth. We investigate the factors contributing to this record-breaking heat and the potential repercussions for both natural ecosystems and human populations worldwide.

Section 4: Accelerating Climate Events

In this section, we focus on the increasing frequency and intensity of extreme weather events, such as hurricanes, heatwaves, droughts, and wildfires, as undeniable signs of global boiling. We analyze the link between human activities and these catastrophic occurrences.

Section 5: Consequences for Biodiversity

The implications of global boiling extend far beyond temperature records. We explore its impact on biodiversity, examining how rising temperatures and habitat loss are pushing many species to the brink of extinction. We also highlight the interconnectedness of ecosystems and the potential cascade effects on the entire biosphere.

Section 6: A Wake-Up Call for Humanity

In the final part of this chapter, we reflect on the moral imperative facing humanity in the face of global boiling. We discuss how this environmental crisis affects vulnerable communities disproportionately and the responsibility of those with power and privilege to drive change.

Conclusion:

Chapter 1 concludes with a call to action, emphasizing the need for immediate and collective efforts to address the challenges of global boiling. We underscore the importance of this new era as a catalyst for global cooperation, innovative solutions, and a renewed commitment to preserving the planet for future generations.

As the world grapples with the intensifying consequences of climate change, a stark declaration echoes across the globe: "The era of global warming has ended; the era of global boiling has arrived." This ominous proclamation by the United Nations Chief, António Guterres, serves as a wake-up call, ushering humanity into a new era where the urgency to address climate change has never been more pressing.

Chapter 2: Unraveling the Causes

Introduction:

As the reality of global boiling sets in, the need to understand its underlying causes becomes paramount. In this chapter, we embark on a journey to unravel the complex web of factors driving this intensified phase of climate change. By exploring the root causes of global boiling, we gain insights into the actions necessary to address and mitigate its impacts.

Section 1: The Greenhouse Effect and Human Influence

At the core of global boiling lies the greenhouse effect, a natural phenomenon that regulates Earth's temperature by trapping a portion of the sun's energy in the atmosphere. We delve into the science of this mechanism and its historical role in sustaining a habitable climate.

However, human activities have dramatically altered this delicate balance. The burning of fossil fuels for energy, deforestation, industrial processes, and agricultural practices release vast amounts of greenhouse gasses into the atmosphere. We analyze how the increased concentrations of carbon dioxide, methane, nitrous oxide, and fluorinated gasses disrupt the natural greenhouse effect, leading to an unnaturally accelerated warming of the planet.

Section 2: Industrialization and Fossil Fuels

Industrialization brought about unprecedented economic growth and technological advancements, but it also marked a turning point in humanity's impact on the climate. We explore the rise of the fossil fuel era and how the combustion of coal, oil, and natural gas became the backbone of global economies.

By examining the expansion of transportation, manufacturing, and energy production fueled by these finite resources, we gain insight into the scale of carbon emissions and their role in propelling us towards global boiling. We also discuss the challenges and opportunities associated with transitioning to cleaner and more sustainable energy sources.

Section 3: Deforestation and Land Use Change

The world's forests have served as crucial carbon sinks, absorbing large amounts of carbon dioxide from the atmosphere. However, rampant deforestation and land use changes, primarily for agriculture and urbanization, have severely compromised their ability to mitigate climate change.

We investigate the consequences of deforestation and the loss of biodiversity, highlighting the role of intact forests in regulating local and global climates. We also explore the potential of reforestation and afforestation efforts to sequester carbon and protect invaluable ecosystems.

Section 4: Methane and Other Potent Greenhouse Gasses

Beyond carbon dioxide, other greenhouse gasses, such as methane and nitrous oxide, contribute significantly to global boiling. We analyze the sources of these potent gasses, including agricultural activities, livestock production, waste management, and natural processes like wetland emissions.

Understanding the impact of these gasses is crucial for developing targeted strategies to reduce their emissions and mitigate their warming potential. We discuss innovative solutions for methane capture and management, as well as the importance of reducing emissions of fluorinated gasses used in various industrial applications.

Section 5: The Role of Land and Oceans

Earth's land and oceans play a vital role in the carbon cycle. We examine how land degradation, including desertification and soil erosion, affects carbon storage capacity and exacerbates climate change. Additionally, we explore the consequences of ocean acidification caused by excessive carbon dioxide absorption, threatening marine ecosystems and the livelihoods of millions who depend on the sea.

Section 6: Amplifying Feedback Loops

Global boiling can trigger self-reinforcing feedback loops, intensifying its effects. We delve into feedback mechanisms such as the albedo effect, where melting ice and snow expose darker surfaces that absorb more heat, accelerating warming. We also explore the potential release of methane from thawing permafrost, further amplifying greenhouse gas concentrations.

Conclusion:

Chapter 2 concludes with a comprehensive understanding of the multifaceted causes driving global boiling. Human activities, driven by industrialization, overreliance on fossil fuels, deforestation, and land-use changes, have fundamentally altered Earth's climate balance. This chapter sets the groundwork for the following sections, where we explore the far-reaching impacts of global boiling on our planet and societies. By grasping the root causes of this crisis, we are better equipped to devise effective and transformative solutions necessary to confront the challenges of global boiling.

Chapter 3: Earth's Hottest Month: A Startling Record

Introduction:

In the relentless march towards global boiling, a chilling milestone is reached. As we delve into the records of our planet's climate history, we confront the reality of July as Earth's hottest month ever recorded. In this chapter, we examine the shocking data that confirms this unprecedented occurrence, shedding light on the rapidly escalating consequences of climate change.

Section 1: Tracking Temperature Trends

We begin by setting the stage for understanding how scientists monitor and record global temperatures. From historic temperature measurements to the advent of modern satellite technology, we explore the methodologies employed to track temperature trends on a global scale.

Through meticulous analysis of temperature data from diverse sources, scientists have detected a concerning pattern of warming that stretches across the globe. We investigate the key findings and conclusions from these data sets, revealing the rapid rise in average global temperatures over the past decades.

Section 2: A New Climatic Record

In this section, we focus on the specific data that revealed July as the hottest month on record. We analyze the measurements and assessments made by various climate monitoring agencies and research institutions worldwide.

The data indicate a remarkable increase in temperature anomalies, surpassing all previous records. We delve into the regions that experienced the most substantial warming and explore the implications of these soaring temperatures on both human populations and ecosystems.

Section 3: Consequences of Record-Breaking Heat

The repercussions of Earth's hottest month reverberate throughout the natural world. We investigate the immediate and long-term consequences of this extreme heat on the planet's delicate balance.

From prolonged and deadly heat waves that threaten human health and agricultural productivity to the escalation of wildfires that engulf vast landscapes, we uncover the devastating impact of extreme heat events. We also discuss how hotter temperatures interact with other climate factors, such as precipitation patterns, and influence weather extremes.

Section 4: Rising Sea Levels and Melting Glaciers

In this section, we turn our attention to the cryosphere - Earth's frozen regions - and the consequences of Earth's hottest month on these critical ice reserves. We explore the acceleration of glacial melting, both in the polar regions and mountain ranges, and the subsequent implications for sea-level rise.

As ice sheets lose mass and glaciers retreat, we discuss the threats posed to coastal communities and low-lying regions. Rising sea levels exacerbate the impacts of storm surges and tidal flooding, endangering millions of people living in vulnerable areas.

Section 5: Ecosystem Vulnerability

Earth's hottest month also places immense strain on ecosystems worldwide. We examine the effects of extreme heat on terrestrial and marine environments, including coral reefs, forests, and fragile habitats.

The chapter delves into the consequences of heat stress on biodiversity, including the bleaching of coral reefs and disruptions in migratory patterns. We also investigate how altered climate conditions affect ecosystems' ability to provide vital ecosystem services, from regulating the water cycle to supporting pollinators and natural pest control.

Section 6: The Human Toll

Amid the grim data and ecological impacts, we cannot overlook the human toll of Earth's hottest month. We explore the far-reaching consequences for human health, agriculture, and livelihoods, particularly in regions already facing climate vulnerability.

Extreme heat puts vulnerable populations at greater risk, including the elderly, children, and those without access to adequate cooling and resources. We delve into the socioeconomic implications, including impacts on food security, water resources, and livelihoods in vulnerable regions.

Conclusion:

Chapter 3 concludes with a somber realization of the profound impact of Earth's hottest month. This record-breaking event serves as an urgent reminder of the reality of global boiling and its devastating consequences for both nature and humanity.

As temperatures continue to rise, the urgency to address the root causes of climate change and implement adaptation and mitigation measures becomes more critical than ever. The data presented in this chapter underscore the need for immediate and collective action to safeguard our planet and its inhabitants from the unfolding crisis of global boiling.

Chapter 4: The Impact on Our Planet's Ecosystems

Introduction:

In this chapter, we delve into the far-reaching consequences of global boiling on Earth's intricate web of ecosystems. As temperatures soar and climate patterns shift, natural habitats and biodiversity face unprecedented challenges. From fragile coral reefs to expansive forests, we explore how these vital ecosystems are being fundamentally altered and threatened by the intensifying impacts of climate change.

Section 1: Coral Reefs in Peril

Coral reefs, among the most diverse and productive ecosystems on the planet, are particularly vulnerable to the effects of global boiling. We examine the phenomenon of coral bleaching, a consequence of rising sea temperatures and ocean acidification, which poses an existential threat to these intricate underwater ecosystems.

Through in-depth case studies, we illustrate how coral bleaching events are becoming more frequent and severe, leading to widespread reef degradation and loss of biodiversity. We also explore the implications of coral reef decline on coastal communities, fishing industries, and the broader marine ecosystem.

Section 2: Forests Under Siege

Forests, often referred to as the lungs of the Earth, play a vital role in sequestering carbon dioxide and regulating the global climate. However, they are facing unprecedented challenges due to global boiling. We investigate the impact of extreme heat, prolonged droughts, and increasing incidence of wildfires on forest health and resilience.

Drawing on evidence from diverse forest ecosystems, including tropical rainforests and boreal forests, we analyze the consequences of deforestation and the disruption of natural forest regeneration processes. Additionally, we explore the feedback loops created by forest degradation, as reduced carbon sequestration contributes to further warming.

Section 3: Disruption in Ocean Ecosystems

The warming oceans present a formidable threat to marine ecosystems. We delve into the impacts of rising sea temperatures on marine life, including shifts in species distribution, altered migration patterns, and disruptions in food chains.

From the decline of iconic marine species to the loss of critical habitats like kelp forests and seagrass beds, we highlight the consequences of these changes on marine biodiversity and fisheries. Moreover, we discuss the implications of ocean acidification, which not only affects coral reefs but also poses risks to shell-forming organisms and marine food webs.

Section 4: Alpine Ecosystems at the Brink

High-altitude ecosystems, such as alpine regions and mountain ranges, are also grappling with the consequences of global boiling. We explore how rising temperatures are causing the retreat of glaciers, affecting the availability of freshwater resources that millions of people depend on.

The chapter investigates how these changes impact alpine flora and fauna, as well as the cultural and socioeconomic significance of these ecosystems for mountain communities. Additionally, we address the implications of melting permafrost and the potential release of methane, contributing to further warming.

Section 5: Vulnerability of Wetlands and Coastal Areas

Wetlands and coastal areas face compounding threats from global boiling, including sea-level rise, storm surges, and altered precipitation patterns. We examine how these changes impact the delicate balance of wetland ecosystems, affecting water purification, flood control, and biodiversity.

Furthermore, we investigate the risks posed to coastal communities as rising sea levels erode coastlines, leading to habitat loss and increased vulnerability to extreme weather events. The loss of mangroves, salt marshes, and other coastal habitats also has significant implications for coastal protection and climate resilience.

Conclusion:

Chapter 4 concludes with a sobering look at the profound impact of global boiling on our planet's ecosystems. Coral reefs, forests, oceans, alpine regions, wetlands, and coastlines are all undergoing rapid changes that threaten their integrity and ecological functions.

The transformation of these ecosystems not only affects the flora and fauna that call them home but also has far-reaching consequences for human societies, economies, and well-being. The evidence presented in this chapter reinforces the urgency for comprehensive action to mitigate climate change and protect the invaluable ecosystems that sustain life on Earth. Without immediate and collective efforts to address global boiling, the consequences for biodiversity, food security, water resources, and countless livelihoods will be irreparable.

Chapter 5: Humanity Under Pressure: Societal Effects

Introduction:

As global boiling intensifies, its far-reaching impacts extend beyond the natural world to profoundly affect human societies. In this chapter, we explore the various societal effects of climate change, from exacerbating existing vulnerabilities to posing new challenges that test our resilience and ability to adapt. From displacement and migration to economic disruptions, we examine how humanity is under pressure to confront the multifaceted consequences of this accelerating crisis.

Section 1: Climate-Induced Migration and Displacement

One of the most significant societal impacts of global boiling is the forced migration and displacement of communities. We investigate the phenomenon of climate-induced migration, where rising sea levels, extreme weather events, and environmental degradation compel people to abandon their homes and seek safer ground.

Drawing on case studies from regions vulnerable to these climate impacts, we explore the human stories behind climate-induced displacement. From small island nations facing existential threats to coastal communities grappling with the loss of their land, we highlight the pressing need for coordinated efforts to support climate refugees and build climate-resilient communities.

Section 2: Food Insecurity and Water Stress

Global boiling poses severe challenges to food and water security worldwide. We analyze the impact of changing climate patterns on agriculture, such as shifts in growing seasons, altered precipitation, and increased frequency of extreme weather events like droughts and floods.

In regions heavily reliant on rain-fed agriculture, we explore the risks of crop failures and food shortages, and how these challenges disproportionately affect vulnerable populations. Additionally, we investigate the growing stress on water resources, including aquifer depletion and the shrinking availability of freshwater for agricultural, industrial, and domestic use.

Section 3: Economic Disruptions and Inequality

The economic ramifications of global boiling are vast and complex. We delve into how climate-related events, such as hurricanes, wildfires, and extreme heat waves, disrupt economies, leading to significant financial losses and increased social inequalities.

We explore the disproportionate impact on low-income communities, who often bear the brunt of climate-related disasters and have limited resources to recover and rebuild. Additionally, we analyze the challenges faced by businesses and industries grappling with climate risks and the necessity for climate-resilient economic policies.

Section 4: Health and Well-being

Global boiling has profound effects on human health and well-being. We examine the direct and indirect health impacts of extreme heat, air pollution, and the spread of vector-borne diseases, such as malaria and dengue, as climate change expands the geographic range of disease vectors.

Furthermore, we address the mental health toll of climate-induced disasters and long-term environmental changes, highlighting the need for psychological support and resilience-building strategies for affected communities.

Section 5: Social and Political Dynamics

The societal effects of global boiling also manifest in social and political dynamics. We explore how climate change exacerbates existing social tensions and inequalities, leading to potential conflicts over resources and migration.

We investigate the role of climate change in shaping political agendas and international relations, from climate diplomacy to the rise of climate activism and international climate agreements. Additionally, we discuss the importance of inclusive climate policy-making that considers diverse perspectives and fosters global cooperation.

Conclusion:

Chapter 5 concludes by underscoring the profound societal effects of global boiling. As climate change intertwines with various aspects of human life, from migration and food security to health and social dynamics, the urgency to address this crisis becomes undeniable.

To build a more resilient and equitable future, comprehensive strategies are needed to mitigate climate impacts, support vulnerable communities, and adapt to the inevitable changes ahead. It is essential for societies to recognize the interconnectedness of global challenges and unite in collective action to confront the human toll of global boiling. Only through solidarity, cooperation, and innovative solutions can we navigate the societal pressures brought about by the intensifying impacts of climate change.

Chapter 6: Tipping Points and Potential Scenarios

Introduction:

In the journey to understand the gravity of global boiling, we encounter the concept of tipping points - critical thresholds beyond which irreversible and abrupt changes may occur. In this chapter, we delve into the intricate science of tipping points, examining potential scenarios that could unfold if these thresholds are crossed. Understanding these tipping points is crucial for grasping the urgency of our actions and the need to prevent catastrophic outcomes.

Section 1: The Science of Tipping Points

We begin by exploring the scientific basis of tipping points in Earth's climate system. Drawing on research from climate science, we explain how certain feedback loops, such as the release of methane from permafrost or the disintegration of ice shelves, can amplify warming and push the climate towards tipping points.

We examine the implications of surpassing these tipping points, which may trigger nonlinear and cascading effects, potentially leading to widespread disruption of ecosystems, weather patterns, and human societies. We also discuss the challenges in predicting precisely when and where tipping points may occur, underscoring the importance of precautionary action.

Section 2: Melting Ice and Rising Seas

One of the most alarming tipping points is the destabilization of polar ice sheets. We investigate the potential scenarios if ice loss in Antarctica and Greenland accelerates, contributing to a significant rise in sea levels.

We explore how sea-level rise, combined with intensified storm surges and tidal flooding, could lead to the inundation of coastal areas, displacing millions of people and threatening critical infrastructure. Additionally, we discuss the impacts on small island nations, which may face the risk of becoming uninhabitable due to rising seas.

Section 3: Disrupting Ocean Circulation

The ocean plays a crucial role in regulating the planet's climate through its complex circulation patterns. We examine the possibility of tipping points in ocean circulation, such as the weakening of the Atlantic Meridional Overturning Circulation (AMOC).

We investigate the potential consequences of a disrupted AMOC, including altered weather patterns, regional cooling in some areas, and warming in others. We also discuss the implications for marine ecosystems, fisheries, and weather extremes in different regions worldwide.

Section 4: Ecosystem Collapse

Tipping points in ecological systems pose a significant threat to biodiversity and food security. We delve into potential scenarios where ecosystems reach tipping points, leading to rapid loss of species and ecosystem services.

Through case studies, we explore how the collapse of critical ecosystems, such as the Amazon rainforest or the Great Barrier Reef, would have profound impacts on global climate regulation, food production, and cultural heritage. We discuss the urgent need for conservation efforts and measures to prevent ecosystem tipping points.

Section 5: Feedback Loops and Amplifying Effects

The interconnectedness of climate systems may lead to the amplification of warming effects. We examine feedback loops that could escalate global boiling, such as the albedo effect and the release of greenhouse gasses from thawing permafrost.

We analyze how feedback loops can create self-reinforcing cycles of warming, making it even more challenging to halt climate change once certain thresholds are surpassed. Understanding these feedback mechanisms reinforces the importance of swift and ambitious climate action.

Conclusion:

Chapter 6 concludes with a sobering assessment of the potential scenarios associated with tipping points in a world experiencing global boiling. The risks of crossing critical thresholds demand immediate and coordinated action on an unprecedented scale.

The evidence presented underscores the necessity of limiting global warming to mitigate the likelihood of triggering these tipping points. Through collective efforts to reduce greenhouse gas emissions, invest in sustainable technologies, and prioritize conservation, we can strive to safeguard against catastrophic outcomes and build a more resilient and stable future for humanity and the planet. The urgency is clear - the time for action is now.

Chapter 7: Unmasking Human Activities

Introduction:

In this chapter, we unmask the undeniable role of human activities as the primary driver of global boiling. Through centuries of industrialization and overconsumption, our species has significantly altered the Earth's climate and ecosystems. As we delve into the various human activities responsible for climate change, we confront the profound responsibility we bear in charting the course towards a sustainable and resilient future.

Section 1: The Burning of Fossil Fuels

At the heart of human-induced climate change lies the burning of fossil fuels - coal, oil, and natural gas. We delve into the historical roots of our dependence on these non-renewable resources and the unparalleled energy revolution they facilitated.

We explore how the combustion of fossil fuels releases vast amounts of carbon dioxide into the atmosphere, leading to the greenhouse effect and global warming. From powering our industries to fueling transportation and electricity generation, we analyze the pervasive influence of fossil fuels in shaping modern life.

Section 2: Industrialization and Carbon Footprint

The growth of industrialization has brought unparalleled economic progress but at a tremendous environmental cost. We investigate the carbon footprint of industrial processes, including manufacturing, cement production, and chemical industries.

Through case studies, we examine how industries contribute to carbon emissions, air pollution, and ecological degradation. We also discuss how sustainable practices, technological advancements, and circular economy models offer pathways towards greener industries.

Section 3: Deforestation and Land Use Change

The clearing of forests for agriculture, urban expansion, and resource extraction has transformed vast landscapes, leading to deforestation and land use change. We explore the global impact of deforestation and its consequences for climate change, biodiversity loss, and carbon sequestration.

We investigate the importance of preserving intact forests and adopting sustainable land management practices to mitigate climate change and protect ecosystems. Additionally, we discuss the role of reforestation and afforestation initiatives in combating global boiling.

Section 4: Agriculture and Livestock Production

The global demand for food and animal products has driven extensive changes in land use and agricultural practices. We examine how agriculture contributes to greenhouse gas emissions through activities such as rice cultivation, the use of synthetic fertilizers, and livestock production.

By delving into sustainable agricultural practices and the potential of regenerative agriculture, we explore how food systems can transition towards climate-resilient and environmentally-friendly models.

Section 5: Waste Management and Pollution

Waste management and pollution further compound the impact of human activities on the environment and climate. We analyze the consequences of improper waste disposal, plastic pollution, and the release of methane from landfills.

We discuss the importance of adopting circular economy approaches, waste reduction strategies, and innovative recycling methods to minimize environmental harm and contribute to a circular, zero-waste society.

Conclusion:

Chapter 7 concludes by laying bare the undeniable evidence of human activities as the root cause of global boiling. From burning fossil fuels to deforestation and unsustainable agriculture, we are leaving an indelible mark on the planet.

The chapter emphasizes that recognizing our role in climate change is not a burden but an opportunity for transformation and progress. By unmasking our actions, we can embrace sustainable alternatives, innovative technologies, and global cooperation to address the challenges of global boiling. Only through collective efforts can we redirect our trajectory and forge a path towards a more sustainable and resilient future for all life on Earth.

Chapter 8: The Role of Industrialization and Fossil Fuels

Introduction:

In this chapter, we delve deeper into the pivotal role of industrialization and fossil fuels in driving global boiling. The transformative power of industrialization has reshaped human societies and economies, but it has also unleashed a cascade of environmental consequences. We explore how our reliance on fossil fuels for energy production and industrial processes has been the primary catalyst for the alarming rise in greenhouse gas emissions, leading to the climate crisis we face today.

Section 1: Industrial Revolution and its Impact

We begin by examining the historical context of the Industrial Revolution, which marked a turning point in human history. We analyze how innovations in machinery, transportation, and manufacturing during the 18th and 19th centuries laid the foundation for the modern industrial society we live in.

We also investigate the exponential increase in energy consumption as a result of industrialization and how this growing demand led to the widespread use of fossil fuels as the primary energy source.

Section 2: The Dominance of Fossil Fuels

Fossil fuels, including coal, oil, and natural gas, have become the lifeblood of modern economies. We delve into their extraction, transportation, and usage across various sectors, from electricity generation to transportation and industrial processes.

Drawing on energy consumption data, we illustrate the overwhelming share of fossil fuels in the global energy mix and the corresponding rise in greenhouse gas emissions.

Section 3: Greenhouse Gas Emissions and Global Warming

The burning of fossil fuels releases large quantities of greenhouse gasses into the atmosphere, including carbon dioxide (CO2), methane (CH4), and nitrous oxide (N2O). We examine the role of these gasses in trapping heat and causing the greenhouse effect, leading to global warming.

By analyzing historical records of atmospheric CO2 concentrations and temperature trends, we establish the link between industrialization, fossil fuel usage, and the unprecedented rise in global temperatures.

Section 4: Deforestation and Industrialization

Industrialization has also spurred deforestation and land use change to make way for agriculture, urbanization, and industrial expansion. We explore how clearing forests for agricultural land and timber resources disrupts the carbon cycle, reducing the Earth's capacity to absorb CO2.

We investigate the implications of deforestation on biodiversity, ecosystem services, and climate regulation. Additionally, we discuss the role of sustainable land management and reforestation efforts in mitigating climate change.

Section 5: The Carbon Budget and Unburnable Fossil Fuels

The concept of the carbon budget is essential in understanding the urgency of reducing fossil fuel usage. We examine how the Earth's atmosphere can only absorb a limited amount of CO2 before surpassing dangerous warming thresholds.

We explore the concept of "unburnable fossil fuels," referring to the need to leave a significant portion of known fossil fuel reserves untapped to prevent catastrophic climate change. We discuss the challenges and opportunities in transitioning to cleaner, renewable energy sources to stay within the carbon budget.

Conclusion:

Chapter 8 concludes by underscoring the integral role of industrialization and fossil fuels in shaping the current climate crisis. As industrialization propelled humanity into a new era of economic growth, it simultaneously set in motion the chain of events leading to global boiling.

Recognizing the link between human activities, fossil fuel usage, and climate change is crucial in developing effective strategies to address global warming and transition towards sustainable energy systems. By adopting clean energy technologies, embracing energy efficiency, and reevaluating our consumption patterns, we can pave the way for a more resilient and climate-friendly future. The challenge lies in harnessing the power of industrialization to drive a global transformation that safeguards the planet for future generations.

Chapter 9: Amplifying Feedback Loops

Introduction:

In this chapter, we explore the intricate interplay of feedback loops in the context of global boiling. Feedback loops are self-reinforcing mechanisms that can amplify the effects of climate change, creating a cascade of consequences that exacerbate the warming process. By understanding these feedback loops, we gain insight into the urgency of addressing global warming and the importance of preventing further escalation of climate impacts.

Section 1: Positive and Negative Feedbacks

Feedback loops can be either positive or negative, depending on their impact on the climate system. We delve into the distinction between these two types of feedback loops and how they interact to shape the Earth's climate.

Positive feedback loops amplify the initial change, leading to further warming or cooling. We focus on the positive feedbacks that are currently driving global boiling, such as the albedo effect, permafrost thawing, and the release of methane and carbon dioxide from natural sources.

Section 2: The Albedo Effect

The albedo effect refers to the reflectivity of the Earth's surface. We examine how melting ice, snow, and glaciers reduce the planet's albedo, as darker surfaces absorb more sunlight and heat up.

By analyzing the consequences of declining ice cover in the Arctic and Antarctic regions, we explore the rapid changes occurring in these polar ecosystems and the potential implications for global temperatures.

Section 3: Permafrost Thaw and Methane Release

Permafrost is permanently frozen ground that contains vast amounts of organic matter. As temperatures rise, permafrost begins to thaw, releasing methane, a potent greenhouse gas.

We investigate the impact of permafrost thawing on greenhouse gas concentrations and the potential for a feedback loop, where increased methane emissions lead to further warming. We also discuss the significance of monitoring and mitigating permafrost-related emissions.

Section 4: Ocean Acidification and Carbon Uptake

The oceans play a crucial role in absorbing carbon dioxide from the atmosphere. However, this process also leads to ocean acidification, as the increased CO_2 concentration alters the water's chemistry.

We explore the implications of ocean acidification on marine ecosystems and the potential for negative feedback loops, where stressed marine life may reduce their ability to sequester carbon, further amplifying atmospheric CO_2 levels.

Section 5: Water Vapor Feedback

Water vapor is the most abundant greenhouse gas in the atmosphere, and its concentration increases with higher temperatures. We investigate the role of water vapor in amplifying the greenhouse effect and its potential to intensify climate change.

By examining the link between rising temperatures, atmospheric water vapor, and extreme weather events, we explore the complex relationship between water vapor and global boiling.

Section 6: Human-Induced Feedbacks

In addition to natural feedback loops, human activities can also contribute to amplifying climate change. We discuss the human-induced feedback arising from deforestation, land use changes, and emissions from industrial processes and transportation.

We analyze the potential for mitigating human-induced feedback through sustainable land management, reforestation efforts, and transitioning to low-carbon technologies.

Conclusion:

Chapter 9 concludes by underlining the significance of feedback loops in accelerating global boiling. These complex interactions between natural and human-induced feedback underscore the urgency of reducing greenhouse gas emissions and adopting sustainable practices.

By identifying and understanding these feedback mechanisms, we can take targeted actions to break the cycle of amplification and work towards a more stable and resilient climate. Addressing feedback loops is essential in charting a sustainable path towards a future where the impacts of global warming are mitigated, and the planet's ecosystems and communities are safeguarded for generations to come.

Chapter 10: Confronting Climate Change Denial

Introduction:

In this chapter, we address the challenge of climate change denial and explore the importance of acknowledging the overwhelming scientific consensus on global boiling. Despite the scientific evidence supporting human-induced climate change, a vocal minority continues to cast doubt on its existence and consequences. We delve into the origins and tactics of climate change denial and discuss the crucial role of communication, education, and collective action in overcoming this obstacle to climate action.

Section 1: The Scientific Consensus

We begin by presenting the unequivocal scientific consensus on climate change. We examine the extensive research conducted by climate scientists worldwide, and the multiple lines of evidence that support the understanding of anthropogenic global warming.

Through a comprehensive review of major scientific reports and assessments, we establish unanimity among climate experts regarding the reality of global boiling and its far-reaching impacts on the environment and human societies.

Section 2: Origins and Tactics of Climate Change Denial

We investigate the origins of climate change denial and how it has been perpetuated by certain interest groups and industries. We explore how misinformation campaigns and cherry-picked data have been used to sow doubt about climate science.

By analyzing the tactics employed by climate change deniers, we shed light on how these strategies have been used to create confusion, delay climate action, and protect vested interests.

Section 3: Psychological and Cultural Factors

Climate change denial often stems from psychological and cultural factors. We delve into the psychology behind denial, including cognitive biases, motivated reasoning, and the tendency to discount distant or abstract threats.

Furthermore, we examine how cultural beliefs and political ideologies can influence one's acceptance or rejection of climate science. Understanding these factors is crucial in designing effective communication strategies that resonate with diverse audiences.

Section 4: Communicating Climate Science

In this section, we explore the importance of clear and effective communication in conveying the urgency of climate change. We discuss the challenges in conveying complex scientific information to the general public and policymakers.

We investigate successful communication approaches, including visual storytelling, relatable narratives, and community engagement, that can foster a deeper understanding of climate change and encourage collective action.

Section 5: Education and Climate Literacy

Education plays a critical role in addressing climate change denial and building climate literacy. We explore the need for comprehensive climate education in schools and universities, ensuring that future generations are equipped with the knowledge and tools to address global boiling.

We discuss the role of educators in fostering critical thinking and scientific inquiry, enabling students to make informed decisions about climate-related issues.

Section 6: Overcoming Denial and Building Consensus

Confronting climate change denial requires a collective effort from individuals, communities, and governments. We discuss the importance of creating spaces for constructive dialogue and finding common ground to address climate challenges.

We investigate the potential for bipartisan and international cooperation in tackling global warming, emphasizing the urgency of transcending political divides for the sake of the planet's future.

Conclusion:

Chapter 10 concludes with the recognition that climate change denial poses a significant obstacle to effective climate action. By acknowledging the scientific consensus, addressing psychological and cultural factors, and prioritizing climate education, we can work towards overcoming denial and fostering a collective commitment to combat global boiling.

Ultimately, confronting climate change denial is not only about dispelling misinformation but also about fostering a sense of shared responsibility and stewardship for the Earth. Only through inclusive and informed action can we collectively address the climate crisis and create a sustainable and resilient future for ourselves and future generations.

Chapter 11: Adapting to an Altered World

Introduction:

In this chapter, we explore the imperative of adaptation in the face of an altered world due to global boiling. As the impacts of climate change become increasingly evident, societies and ecosystems must adjust to new realities. We delve into the concept of climate adaptation, its importance in building resilience, and the multifaceted strategies required to confront the challenges posed by a rapidly changing climate.

Section 1: Embracing the Reality of Climate Change

We begin by acknowledging the reality of global boiling and its irreversible consequences. We discuss the importance of accepting the current and projected impacts of climate change to inform effective adaptation measures.

By understanding the different scales and levels of climate change impacts, we emphasize the need for adaptation strategies that are tailored to local and regional contexts.

Section 2: Assessing Vulnerabilities and Risks

Assessing vulnerabilities and risks is crucial in planning adaptation efforts. We examine the methodologies used to identify vulnerable communities, critical infrastructure, and ecosystems susceptible to climate impacts.

We discuss the significance of incorporating future climate projections and scenario planning to inform adaptive decision-making and prioritize areas with the highest risks.

Section 3: Building Climate-Resilient Infrastructure

Climate resilience requires reevaluating the design and construction of infrastructure. We explore the importance of building climate-resilient cities, transportation systems, and buildings that can withstand extreme weather events and changing climate conditions.

We discuss the integration of nature-based solutions, such as green infrastructure and sustainable urban planning, in enhancing climate resilience.

Section 4: Safeguarding Ecosystems and Biodiversity

Ecosystems are vital buffers against climate impacts, but they too face vulnerabilities. We investigate the importance of preserving and restoring ecosystems, such as wetlands, forests, and coastal habitats, to support biodiversity and protect against climate-related disasters.

We discuss the potential of ecological restoration and conservation efforts in bolstering ecosystem resilience and fostering ecological connectivity.

Section 5: Adapting Agriculture and Food Systems

Agriculture and food systems are among the most sensitive sectors to climate change. We explore adaptive farming practices, crop diversification, and water management strategies to cope with changing weather patterns and water availability.

We discuss the importance of supporting smallholder farmers and empowering communities to build climate-resilient food systems.

Section 6: Enhancing Climate Preparedness and Early Warning Systems

Early warning systems and climate preparedness are vital components of adaptation. We investigate the role of meteorological agencies and disaster management authorities in providing timely information and response plans for extreme weather events.

We explore how climate services can assist vulnerable communities in making informed decisions and preparing for climate-related hazards.

Climate adaptation must be guided by principles of social equity and justice. We discuss the importance of including marginalized and vulnerable populations in decision-making processes and ensuring that adaptation efforts do not exacerbate existing inequalities.

We investigate how climate justice can be central to adaptation policies and how communities can be empowered to lead and participate in their resilience-building initiatives.

Conclusion:

Chapter 11 concludes by emphasizing the urgency of adaptation as a fundamental response to the altered world of global boiling. As climate change impacts intensify, adaptation becomes an imperative for safeguarding lives, ecosystems, and economies.

By embracing climate reality, assessing vulnerabilities, and implementing climate-resilient strategies, societies can build the capacity to thrive in the face of change. The challenge of adaptation is complex, but by working collectively and prioritizing climate justice, we can create a world that is better prepared to face the challenges of an uncertain future shaped by climate change.

Chapter 12: Global Boiling and Food Security

Introduction:

In this chapter, we delve into the critical connection between global boiling and food security. Climate change poses significant risks to agriculture and food production systems, threatening food availability, access, and stability. We explore the complex and multifaceted impacts of global warming on food security, and the urgent need for adaptive strategies to ensure a resilient and sustainable food future for a growing global population.

Section 1: Climate Change and Crop Yields

Climate change affects crop yields through changing temperature and precipitation patterns. We investigate the impact of rising temperatures on crop growth, flowering, and fruiting, as well as the consequences of increased frequency and intensity of extreme weather events like droughts and floods.

We discuss the varying regional impacts on major staple crops, such as wheat, rice, and maize, and how climate-induced yield reductions can have far-reaching consequences on food availability and prices.

Section 2: Shifts in Agricultural Zones and Growing Seasons

Global boiling leads to shifts in agricultural zones and growing seasons. We explore how changing climate conditions may expand or contract suitable areas for crop cultivation, affecting crop choices and agricultural practices.

We discuss the implications of these shifts for smallholder farmers and subsistence agriculture, and the importance of adaptive measures to enable farmers to adapt to changing conditions.

Section 3: Water Scarcity and Irrigation Challenges

Water scarcity is one of the most pressing challenges exacerbated by climate change. We investigate the impact of changing precipitation patterns and shrinking water resources on irrigation, a crucial component of modern agriculture.

We explore the need for water-efficient irrigation techniques, water storage solutions, and the role of climate-resilient water management in safeguarding food production.

Section 4: Impact on Livestock and Fisheries

Global boiling also affects livestock and fisheries, integral components of food systems. We analyze the consequences of extreme heat stress on livestock productivity and the potential risks of disease outbreaks.

We discuss the impact of warming oceans on marine ecosystems, fish stocks, and coastal communities dependent on fisheries for food and livelihoods.

Section 5: Food Price Volatility and Access

Climate change-induced disruptions in agriculture can lead to food price volatility, affecting food access for vulnerable populations. We investigate the links between food price spikes, economic stability, and social unrest.

We discuss the importance of social safety nets and food assistance programs in ensuring food access during periods of food insecurity.

Section 6: The Role of Climate-Resilient Agriculture

Adapting agriculture to climate change is essential for ensuring food security. We explore the concept of climate-resilient agriculture, encompassing sustainable practices, crop breeding for resilience, and agroecological approaches.

We discuss the significance of investing in research, extension services, and technology transfer to support farmers in adopting climate-resilient practices.

Section 7: Climate Policies and Global Cooperation

Addressing food security in a changing climate requires strong climate policies and global cooperation. We investigate the importance of integrating food security considerations into climate adaptation and mitigation strategies.

We discuss the role of international cooperation in supporting climate-resilient agriculture, technology transfer, and knowledge sharing among countries.

Conclusion:

Chapter 12 concludes by underscoring the urgency of addressing the complex relationship between global boiling and food security. Climate change poses formidable challenges to agricultural systems, livelihoods, and the well-being of millions.

By prioritizing climate-resilient agriculture, sustainable water management, and social equity, we can work towards ensuring food security for current and future generations. It is essential for governments, policymakers, and communities worldwide to collaborate on adaptive strategies that build resilience and confront the unprecedented challenges posed by global boiling to safeguard the most basic human need - access to food.

Chapter 13: The Race Against Rising Seas

Introduction:

In this chapter, we explore the urgent race against rising seas, one of the most tangible and pressing consequences of global boiling. As temperatures rise and ice sheets melt, sea levels continue to climb, posing unprecedented threats to coastal communities, economies, and ecosystems. We delve into the causes and consequences of rising seas, the challenges of adaptation, and the imperative for decisive action to protect vulnerable regions from the encroaching tides.

Section 1: Understanding Sea Level Rise

We begin by examining the scientific basis of sea level rise. We explore the role of melting glaciers and ice sheets, the thermal expansion of seawater, and other contributing factors in the rising sea levels.

Through historical data and projections, we illustrate the accelerating pace of sea level rise and its implications for the future.

Section 2: Threats to Coastal Communities

Rising seas pose severe threats to coastal communities worldwide. We investigate the impacts of sea level rise on coastal erosion, flooding, and saltwater intrusion into freshwater sources.

Through case studies, we highlight the risks faced by densely populated coastal cities and low-lying island nations, whose very existence is at stake.

Section 3: Climate Refugees and Displacement

The race against rising seas leads to climate-induced displacement. We explore the concept of climate refugees, people forced to leave their homes and communities due to the encroachment of the seas.

We discuss the challenges of accommodating and supporting climate migrants, including the need for international cooperation and compassionate policies.

Section 4: Infrastructure and Economic Vulnerabilities

Critical infrastructure in coastal regions is under threat from rising seas. We investigate the risks to ports, roads, power plants, and other key facilities that are essential for local and global economies.

We explore the economic consequences of sea level rise and the importance of investing in resilient infrastructure.

Section 5: Adaptation Strategies and Resilience

Adapting to rising seas requires innovative strategies and resilience-building measures. We discuss the role of nature-based solutions, such as coastal restoration and mangrove protection, in reducing the impact of sea level rise.

We also explore engineered solutions, such as seawalls and levees, and the importance of balanced approaches that consider the ecological and social implications.

Section 6: Collaborative Efforts and Global Cooperation

Addressing rising seas demands collaborative efforts and global cooperation. We investigate the significance of international agreements and initiatives aimed at mitigating the impacts of climate change and supporting vulnerable coastal regions.

We discuss the potential for financial support, technology transfer, and knowledge sharing to assist developing nations facing the challenges of sea level rise.

Section 7: Fostering Public Awareness and Climate Action

Public awareness and climate action are vital in the race against rising seas. We discuss the importance of engaging communities, stakeholders, and policymakers in understanding the urgency of sea level rise and the need for proactive measures.

We explore the role of education and media in communicating the risks and opportunities for climate-resilient coastal development.

Conclusion:

Chapter 13 concludes with the recognition that the race against rising seas is a defining challenge of our time. The consequences of inaction are severe and will disproportionately affect vulnerable communities.

By acknowledging the reality of sea level rise, implementing adaptation strategies, and fostering global cooperation, we can confront this existential threat and build a more resilient future. The race against rising seas requires collective action, innovation, and a shared commitment to safeguarding coastal communities, economies, and ecosystems from the relentless advance of the tides.

Chapter 14: Climate Refugees: A Looming Crisis

Introduction:

In this chapter, we confront the looming crisis of climate refugees - a consequence of global boiling that poses unprecedented challenges to human mobility and international relations. As climate change accelerates and its impacts intensify, millions of people are expected to be displaced from their homes due to rising seas, extreme weather events, desertification, and other climate-induced factors. We explore the human dimension of this crisis, the complexities of defining climate refugees, and the urgent need for global cooperation in addressing the plight of those displaced by the changing climate.

Section 1: The Human Toll of Climate-Induced Displacement

We begin by humanizing the crisis, sharing the stories of individuals and communities already experiencing climate-induced displacement. We examine the physical and psychological toll of leaving one's homeland due to environmental upheavals.

Through case studies and testimonies, we shed light on the unique challenges climate refugees face and the uncertainties they encounter in search of safer grounds.

Section 2: Defining Climate Refugees and Legal Status

Defining climate refugees under international law is a complex task. We explore the limitations of current legal frameworks in recognizing climate-induced displacement and providing adequate protection.

We discuss the importance of expanding legal protections and advocating for the rights of those displaced by climate change.

Section 3: Increasing Numbers and Regional Hotspots

As the impacts of global boiling intensify, the numbers of climate refugees are expected to rise exponentially. We analyze the regions most vulnerable to climate-induced displacement, including low-lying island nations, coastal communities, and drought-prone areas.

We discuss the challenges of accommodating large-scale migration and the potential for regional conflicts over resources and territory.

Section 4: Climate-Induced Conflict and Security Implications

Climate-induced displacement can also exacerbate existing conflicts and create new security challenges. We investigate how competition for resources, displacement-induced tensions, and social unrest can strain already fragile regions.

We discuss the role of climate change in shaping security agendas and the importance of preventive diplomacy and conflict resolution.

Section 5: Adapting Migration Policies and Protection

Countries and international organizations must adapt their migration policies and protection mechanisms to address climate-induced displacement. We examine the potential for climate-related visa programs, temporary protected status, and other avenues for providing refuge.

We explore the need for equitable burden-sharing and responsibility-sharing in assisting climate refugees.

Section 6: Investing in Climate Resilience and Adaptation

Preventing climate-induced displacement requires investing in climate resilience and adaptation measures. We discuss the importance of supporting vulnerable communities through climate-resilient infrastructure, sustainable livelihoods, and nature-based solutions.

By addressing the root causes of climate-induced displacement, we can reduce the need for migration and displacement.

Section 7: Fostering Global Cooperation

Addressing the crisis of climate refugees demands international cooperation and solidarity. We discuss the potential for multilateral agreements, partnerships, and financial support to assist countries hosting climate refugees.

We explore the importance of fostering collaboration and mutual understanding among nations to confront this global challenge.

Conclusion:

Chapter 14 concludes with the recognition that the crisis of climate refugees is not a distant concern but a present reality. The human costs of climate-induced displacement demand immediate attention and action.

By recognizing climate refugees as a global responsibility, engaging in collaborative efforts, and investing in climate resilience, we can mitigate the worst impacts of climate change-induced displacement.

The looming crisis of climate refugees serves as a wake-up call for humanity to confront the urgent need for ambitious climate action and compassionate response mechanisms. Through international solidarity and collective efforts, we can provide hope and dignity to those displaced by climate change, while simultaneously working towards a more sustainable and equitable future for all.

Chapter 15: From Awareness to Action: The Call for Change

Introduction:

In this chapter, we explore the crucial transition from climate awareness to decisive climate action. The reality of global boiling is now widely recognized, and the consequences of inaction are becoming increasingly dire. We delve into the transformative power of individual and collective action, the importance of political will, and the urgency of embracing sustainable practices to mitigate climate change and safeguard the future of our planet.

Section 1: Empowering Individuals and Communities

The journey from awareness to action begins with empowering individuals and communities. We discuss the significance of education, media, and public awareness campaigns in fostering a deeper understanding of climate change and its impacts.

By empowering individuals with knowledge and tools to take climate-friendly actions in their daily lives, we can create a groundswell of collective effort towards change.

Section 2: The Role of Corporate Responsibility

The private sector plays a crucial role in driving change. We explore the growing importance of corporate responsibility and sustainable business practices in reducing greenhouse gas emissions and promoting environmentally-friendly innovations.

We discuss how businesses can integrate climate considerations into their strategies and supply chains, making sustainability a core value.

Section 3: Political Leadership and Policy Initiatives

Political leadership is pivotal in transforming awareness into concrete action. We examine the role of governments in implementing climate policies and regulations that incentivize clean energy adoption, carbon pricing, and emission reduction targets.

We discuss the importance of international cooperation and ambitious commitments to address the global nature of the climate crisis.

Section 4: Investing in Renewable Energy

Transitioning to renewable energy is a critical step in combating global boiling. We investigate the potential of solar, wind, hydro, and other renewable sources in replacing fossil fuels and reducing greenhouse gas emissions.

We explore the significance of investing in renewable energy infrastructure and the economic opportunities it presents.

Section 5: Climate Finance and Green Investments

Climate finance is essential in supporting climate action. We discuss the need for increased funding for climate mitigation and adaptation projects, especially in developing nations facing the brunt of climate change impacts.

We explore the potential for green investments, climate bonds, and public-private partnerships to accelerate the transition towards a low-carbon economy.

Section 6: Sustainable Agriculture and Land Use

Agriculture and land use are vital components of climate action. We examine the potential of sustainable agricultural practices, agroforestry, and reforestation in sequestering carbon and building climate resilience.

We discuss the importance of transforming land use policies to protect natural habitats and foster biodiversity.

Section 7: Global Solidarity and Climate Justice

Addressing global boiling requires global solidarity and climate justice. We discuss the need for developed nations to support developing countries in climate adaptation and technology transfer.

We explore the role of international agreements and forums in fostering collaboration and equitable climate action.

Conclusion:

Chapter 15 concludes with the recognition that the call for change is no longer a choice but a moral imperative. From individual actions to collective efforts, from corporate responsibility to political leadership, the transformation from climate awareness to action demands a united front.

By embracing sustainable practices, investing in renewable energy, and fostering global cooperation, we can overcome the challenges of global boiling and build a more equitable, resilient, and sustainable world.

The time for action is now. Together, we can create a legacy of responsible stewardship, safeguarding the planet for future generations and leaving behind a thriving Earth for all life to flourish. The call for change is a call to protect the most precious gift we have - our planet Earth.

Chapter 16: Individual Responsibility: Steps Towards Sustainability

Introduction:

In this chapter, we focus on the pivotal role of individual responsibility in promoting sustainability and combating global boiling. The actions of each person, no matter how small, collectively contribute to a more sustainable future. We explore practical steps individuals can take in their daily lives to reduce their ecological footprint, embrace eco-friendly practices, and become agents of positive change in the fight against climate change.

Section 1: Understanding Personal Impact

We begin by emphasizing the significance of understanding one's personal impact on the environment. We discuss the carbon footprint, water usage, and waste generation as key metrics to assess individual contributions to climate change.

Through awareness of personal impact, individuals can identify areas for improvement and set sustainability goals.

Section 2: Adopting Sustainable Consumption

Sustainable consumption is at the heart of individual responsibility. We explore the importance of making conscious choices in purchasing products with lower environmental impacts, such as eco-friendly, locally-sourced, and sustainably-produced goods.

We discuss the potential of reducing meat consumption, embracing plant-based diets, and minimizing food waste as transformative steps towards sustainability.

Section 3: Embracing Renewable Energy

Transitioning to renewable energy sources is a critical action in the fight against global boiling. We explore how individuals can adopt renewable energy at the household level, such as installing solar panels or using green energy providers.

We discuss the potential for energy efficiency measures, such as home insulation and energy-saving appliances, in reducing energy consumption.

Section 4: Sustainable Transportation

Transportation choices significantly impact carbon emissions. We investigate the potential for individuals to reduce their carbon footprint through carpooling, using public transportation, biking, or walking whenever possible.

We discuss the importance of considering electric or hybrid vehicles as cleaner alternatives to traditional fossil fuel-powered cars.

Section 5: Reducing, Reusing, and Recycling

The mantra of "reduce, reuse, and recycle" remains fundamental in sustainability efforts. We explore the importance of reducing single-use plastics, reusing items whenever possible, and actively participating in recycling programs.

We discuss the potential for composting organic waste to reduce landfill contributions and enrich soil health.

Section 6: Supporting Sustainable Policies and Businesses

Individuals can influence sustainability beyond personal actions by supporting sustainable policies and businesses. We discuss the importance of voting for environmentally-conscious leaders and advocating for climate-friendly legislation.

We explore how consumer choices, such as supporting companies with robust sustainability practices, can drive positive change.

Section 7: Educating and Inspiring Others

Educating and inspiring others is a powerful multiplier effect in sustainability efforts. We discuss the role of individuals in raising awareness about climate change and promoting sustainable practices within their communities, workplaces, and social circles.

By sharing knowledge, inspiring action, and fostering a culture of sustainability, individuals can create ripple effects that extend far beyond their own actions.

Conclusion:

Chapter 16 concludes by emphasizing the transformative power of individual responsibility in shaping a sustainable future. Each person's choices, actions, and advocacy play a vital role in the collective effort to combat global boiling and preserve the planet for future generations.

By taking practical steps towards sustainability, individuals become catalysts for broader societal and systemic change. Together, we can create a world that thrives on renewable energy, values conservation, and cherishes the delicate balance of nature.

The call for individual responsibility is not an isolated endeavor but a united front towards a more sustainable and resilient planet. Let us embrace our role as stewards of the Earth and work together to build a better world for all living beings.

Chapter 17: The Power of Collective Action

Introduction:

In this chapter, we explore the transformative potential of collective action in addressing the challenges of global boiling. While individual responsibility is crucial, it is through collective efforts and solidarity that we can bring about significant change at local, national, and global levels. We delve into the history of successful collective movements, the importance of building alliances, and the role of grassroots activism in shaping a sustainable and just future for all.

Section 1: Lessons from Past Movements

We begin by drawing inspiration from past collective movements that have driven social and environmental change. From civil rights to women's suffrage to environmental protection, we examine the power of collective action in advancing progressive causes.

By understanding the strategies and successes of historical movements, we can learn valuable lessons for mobilizing in the face of global boiling.

Section 2: Building Alliances and Coalitions

The strength of collective action lies in building alliances and coalitions. We explore the importance of collaboration among diverse stakeholders, including governments, civil society organizations, businesses, and individuals.

We discuss the potential for bridging ideological divides and finding common ground to drive meaningful action.

Section 3: Youth Activism and the Climate Movement

Youth activism has emerged as a powerful force in the climate movement. We investigate the impact of young activists and their call for urgent climate action, as seen in global movements like Fridays for Future.

We explore the significance of youth-led initiatives in holding decision-makers accountable and inspiring broader societal change.

Section 4: Grassroots Movements and Local Impact

Grassroots movements play a pivotal role in driving change from the ground up. We discuss the importance of community-based initiatives, local advocacy, and bottom-up approaches in addressing climate issues specific to different regions.

We explore how grassroots efforts can create a domino effect, spurring larger-scale actions and influencing policy agendas.

Section 5: Environmental Justice and Marginalized Voices

Collective action must prioritize environmental justice and amplify the voices of marginalized communities. We discuss how vulnerable populations often bear the brunt of climate change impacts and how their inclusion is essential in shaping equitable solutions.

We explore the significance of addressing climate action through a lens of inclusivity and social equality.

Section 6: Holding Leaders and Corporations Accountable

Collective action is instrumental in holding leaders and corporations accountable for their climate impacts.

We discuss the potential for public demonstrations, petitions, shareholder activism, and divestment campaigns to pressure decision-makers and businesses to adopt sustainable practices. We explore the role of collective action in demanding transparency and ethical responsibility.

Section 7: Global Climate Strikes and Summits

Global climate strikes and international summits serve as platforms for collective action on a global scale. We discuss how mass mobilization during climate strikes and conferences like COP (Conference of the Parties) can influence policy outcomes and promote urgent climate action.

We explore the significance of global solidarity in addressing the global challenge of global boiling.

Conclusion:

Chapter 17 concludes with the recognition that collective action is a formidable force in confronting the crisis of global boiling. Together, through united efforts, we can push for systemic changes, drive policy reform, and create a world where sustainability and climate justice are at the forefront.

The power of collective action lies in its ability to transcend borders, cultures, and ideologies to advocate for a common cause - safeguarding the planet for future generations. By coming together in collective action, we can rewrite the narrative of global boiling, creating a legacy of resilience, stewardship, and shared responsibility for the Earth we all call home.

Chapter 18: Innovations and Technological Solutions

Introduction:

In this chapter, we explore the critical role of innovations and technological solutions in addressing the challenges posed by global boiling. As the climate crisis intensifies, there is an urgent need for groundbreaking advancements to reduce greenhouse gas emissions, enhance climate resilience, and transition to a sustainable future. We delve into cutting-edge technologies, nature-inspired innovations, and the potential for transformative solutions that can propel humanity towards a low-carbon, climate-resilient world.

Section 1: Advancements in Renewable Energy

Renewable energy remains at the forefront of the fight against global boiling. We examine the latest advancements in solar, wind, geothermal, and tidal power technologies, as well as their increasing affordability and scalability.

We discuss the potential for energy storage solutions, grid modernization, and decentralized energy systems to revolutionize the global energy landscape.

Section 2: Carbon Capture and Negative Emissions Technologies

Carbon capture and negative emissions technologies play a crucial role in removing carbon dioxide from the atmosphere. We explore the different approaches, such as direct air capture, bioenergy with carbon capture and storage (BECCS), and enhanced weathering.

We discuss the potential for large-scale deployment of these technologies to achieve net-zero emissions and mitigate the impacts of past carbon emissions.

Section 3: Nature-Inspired Innovations

Nature-inspired innovations offer valuable insights into sustainable solutions. We investigate biomimicry, where designs and technologies are inspired by nature's resilience and efficiency.

We explore how bio-inspired materials, energy-efficient designs, and ecosystem restoration efforts can contribute to climate resilience and sustainable development.

Section 4: Smart and Resilient Cities

Cities are key players in climate action. We discuss the concept of smart cities, where technology is used to optimize energy use, transportation, and urban planning.

We explore the potential for resilient infrastructure, green spaces, and circular economy practices to create sustainable and livable cities.

Section 5: Climate Data and Predictive Analytics

Climate data and predictive analytics are vital tools in climate adaptation and risk management. We discuss the importance of gathering and analyzing climate data to inform decision-making, disaster preparedness, and climate modeling.

We explore how advanced analytics and artificial intelligence can enhance our understanding of climate patterns and inform proactive measures.

Section 6: Sustainable Agriculture and Food Systems

Technological innovations can revolutionize agriculture and food systems. We discuss precision farming, vertical agriculture, and hydroponics as methods to increase food production while minimizing environmental impact.

We explore the potential of blockchain and other traceability technologies in promoting sustainable supply chains and reducing food waste.

Section 7: Collaborative Research and Development

Collaborative research and development are critical in advancing climate solutions. We discuss the importance of public-private partnerships, international cooperation, and open-source innovations in accelerating progress.

We explore the potential for sharing knowledge and expertise to tackle the global challenge of global boiling.

Conclusion:

Chapter 18 concludes with the recognition that innovations and technological solutions are essential components of the climate action toolkit. By embracing cutting-edge technologies, harnessing the power of nature-inspired innovations, and investing in research and development, humanity can navigate the complexities of global boiling.

The potential for transformative solutions is within reach, but collective action, political will, and global cooperation are crucial in translating innovations into widespread impact.

Through a combination of policy support, private sector commitment, and public engagement, we can usher in a new era of sustainable development, climate resilience, and shared prosperity for present and future generations. The path to a sustainable future lies in harnessing the power of innovation to reshape our relationship with the environment and pave the way for a thriving and resilient planet.

Chapter 19: Climate Justice: Bridging the Gap

Introduction:

In this chapter, we address the vital concept of climate justice and its role in bridging the gap between those most affected by global boiling and those responsible for its causes. Climate change disproportionately impacts vulnerable communities and regions with the least historical contribution to greenhouse gas emissions. We explore the principles of climate justice, the importance of equitable solutions, and the urgent need to address social, economic, and environmental inequalities in the pursuit of a sustainable and just future.

Section 1: Understanding Climate Inequity

We begin by examining the inequities that underpin the climate crisis. We discuss the historical responsibility of industrialized nations for the majority of carbon emissions and their impacts on vulnerable populations.

We explore how climate change exacerbates existing social injustices and disproportionately affects marginalized communities.

Section 2: The Principles of Climate Justice

The principles of climate justice provide a framework for addressing climate change in a fair and equitable manner. We discuss the concepts of historical responsibility, common but differentiated responsibilities, and the polluter-pays principle.

We explore how climate justice calls for cooperation, solidarity, and collective action on a global scale.

Section 3: Intersectionality and Climate Justice

Climate justice intersects with various social justice issues. We discuss how gender, race, class, and other factors intersect with climate change impacts and responses.

We explore the importance of recognizing and addressing these interconnected challenges to achieve inclusive and effective climate solutions.

Section 4: Empowering Vulnerable Communities

Climate justice empowers vulnerable communities to participate in decision-making processes and shape their own climate futures. We discuss the significance of including indigenous peoples, local communities, and marginalized groups in climate planning and policy development.

We explore the potential for community-based solutions and climate resilience building from the bottom-up.

Section 5: Supporting Climate Adaptation and Mitigation

Climate justice demands support for both adaptation and mitigation efforts. We discuss the importance of assisting developing nations in building climate resilience, transitioning to renewable energy, and implementing sustainable practices.

We explore the potential for climate finance and technology transfer in promoting climate justice globally.

Section 6: Fostering Climate Education and Awareness

Climate education and awareness play a vital role in promoting climate justice. We discuss the importance of accessible education on climate change, environmental stewardship, and sustainability.

We explore the potential for climate literacy to empower individuals and communities in making informed decisions.

Section 7: Advocacy for Policy Change

Climate justice requires advocacy for policy change that prioritizes the needs and rights of vulnerable populations. We discuss the potential for grassroots movements, civil society engagement, and advocacy organizations to influence climate policies and hold decision-makers accountable.

We explore how collective action can drive systemic change towards climate justice.

Conclusion:

Chapter 19 concludes with the recognition that climate justice is an ethical and moral imperative. Bridging the gap between the most affected and the responsible is essential in confronting the global boiling crisis.

By centering climate justice in our responses to climate change, we can create solutions that promote fairness, inclusivity, and resilience. It is incumbent upon all stakeholders, from governments and businesses to individuals and civil society, to work together to address the root causes of climate injustice.

By embracing climate justice, we can build a world where no one is left behind in the fight against global boiling, where the burdens and benefits of climate action are shared equitably, and where the vision of a sustainable and just future becomes a reality for all.

Chapter 20: Hope on the Horizon: A Sustainable Future

Introduction:

In this final chapter, we envision a sustainable future that holds the promise of a world united in the fight against global boiling. We explore the transformative power of hope, the potential for collective action, and the significance of embracing sustainable practices to secure a thriving and resilient planet for generations to come. While the challenges of climate change are immense, the seeds of hope and the momentum for change are growing, inspiring a path towards a sustainable future.

Section 1: The Power of Hope

Hope is a catalyst for change. We discuss how hope inspires individuals and communities to take action in the face of global boiling.

We explore the potential for hope to ignite collective movements and drive transformative solutions that address climate change.

Section 2: A Call for Bold Climate Action

Bold climate action is imperative to create a sustainable future. We discuss the importance of setting ambitious emission reduction targets, transitioning to renewable energy, and investing in sustainable infrastructure.We explore the significance of international cooperation and policy commitments in driving systemic change.

Section 3: Resilient and Livable Cities

Cities are hubs of innovation and progress. We discuss how sustainable urban planning, green spaces, and smart technology can create resilient and livable cities that prioritize the well-being of both people and the planet.

We explore the potential for sustainable transportation, affordable housing, and access to green amenities in shaping sustainable urban centers.

Section 4: A Circular Economy

A circular economy offers a transformative approach to production and consumption. We discuss the potential of reducing waste, recycling materials, and adopting sustainable practices that minimize environmental impact.

We explore how circularity fosters economic prosperity while preserving the Earth's resources.

Section 5: Protecting Biodiversity and Ecosystems

Biodiversity is fundamental to the planet's health. We discuss the importance of conserving ecosystems, protecting endangered species, and restoring natural habitats.

We explore the potential of nature-based solutions in combating climate change and enhancing resilience.

Section 6: Empowering Communities and Climate Justice

Sustainable development is inseparable from climate justice. We discuss how empowering communities, especially those most affected by climate change, is essential in shaping equitable solutions.

We explore the potential of inclusive policies, community-led initiatives, and a just transition towards a sustainable future.

Section 7: A Global Commitment to Sustainability

The journey towards a sustainable future requires a global commitment. We discuss the significance of governments, businesses, organizations, and individuals working together to achieve shared goals.

We explore the potential of collaborative efforts, technology transfer, and capacity-building in addressing global boiling.

Conclusion:

Chapter 20 concludes with a message of hope and determination. While the challenges of global boiling are complex and far-reaching, a sustainable future is within reach if we act with urgency and unity.

By embracing the transformative power of hope, adopting bold climate action, and prioritizing sustainability in all aspects of life, we can create a world that thrives on renewable energy, protects biodiversity, and champions climate justice.

The vision of a sustainable future is not an abstract dream but a tangible reality that we can collectively shape. Together, let us embark on this journey towards a sustainable future, where hope, innovation, and determination lead us to a world of prosperity, equity, and resilience for all living beings. The time for action is now, and the future is in our hands.

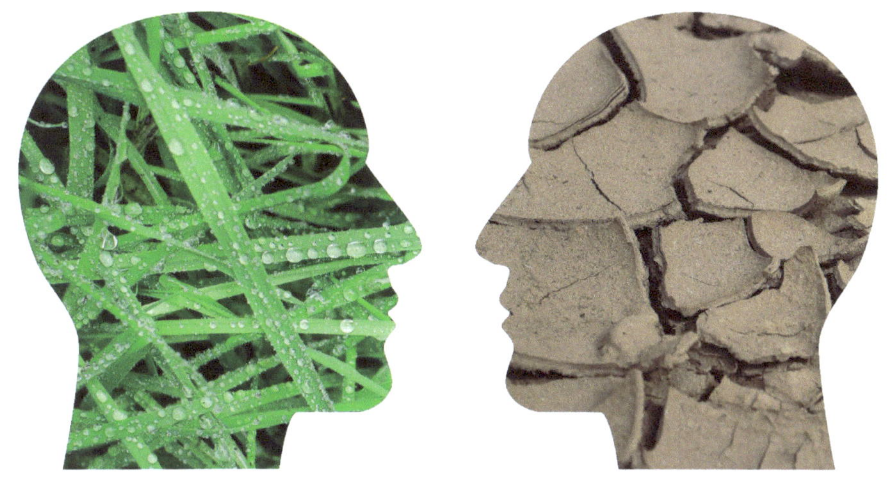

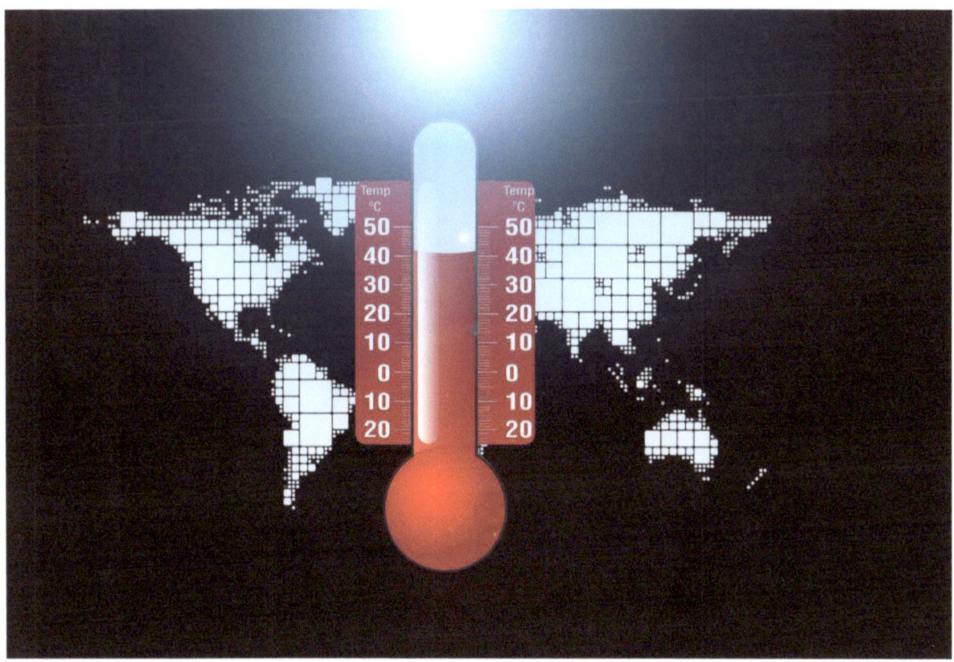

Conclusion:

As we reach the conclusion of this book on global boiling, we stand at a critical crossroads in human history. The era of global warming has given way to the harsh reality of global boiling, a time of unprecedented climate challenges that demand urgent and collective action. Throughout these pages, we have explored the gravity of the climate crisis, the causes and consequences of rising temperatures, and the transformative power of hope, collective action, and innovative solutions.

Global boiling is not an isolated problem; it is a crisis that touches every corner of the globe and affects every living being. It knows no borders, and its impacts spare no one. The rise in temperatures, extreme weather events, sea level rise, and disruptions to ecosystems are symptoms of a planet under stress. But amidst these challenges, we have also discovered a beacon of hope—a growing movement of people determined to secure a sustainable and just future for all.

The call for action is now stronger than ever. Each one of us has a role to play in this defining chapter of human existence. From individuals making conscious choices to governments and corporations embracing sustainable practices, our collective efforts can reshape the trajectory of global boiling. By embracing the principles of climate justice, we can bridge the gap between the most affected and those responsible, ensuring that no one is left behind in this transformative journey.

The road ahead will be difficult, and the solutions complex, but we are not without the means to create change. Innovations in renewable energy, nature-inspired solutions, sustainable agriculture, and advancements in technology are all tools that can propel us towards a sustainable future. By empowering vulnerable communities, promoting climate literacy, and fostering international cooperation, we can overcome the challenges of global boiling together.

We must rise above the barriers of ideology, geography, and self-interest to embrace a shared vision of a sustainable planet. Our actions today will reverberate for generations to come. As we confront the reality of global boiling, we must remember that hope is not lost. It is our most potent ally—a driving force that fuels our determination, ignites our imagination, and propels us towards a future where humanity and nature coexist in harmony.

The journey towards a sustainable future is not a solitary one; it is a collective endeavor that requires the participation of all nations, communities, and individuals. By unifying under the banner of hope and taking decisive climate action, we can create a legacy of stewardship—a testament to our resolve to protect the precious gift of our planet.

Let this book be a call to action—a call to embrace hope, take responsibility, and transform global boiling into an opportunity for a brighter and more sustainable tomorrow. The story of our planet's future is still being written, and the pen is in our hands. Together, let us write a narrative of courage, compassion, and resilience—a story of triumph over adversity and a celebration of our shared humanity. The hope on the horizon is within our reach. Let us seize it and shape a sustainable future for the generations to come.

The author will donate part of the proceeds from the sales of this book but you also can donate to:

Donate below to the UN's Emergency Fund and your money will fund life-saving aid in crises around the world.

@ https://crisisrelief.un.org/donate

HOW YOUR DONATION MAKES A DIFFERENCE

Your donations go directly to relief organizations delivering life-saving aid at the front lines of the world's most severe crises.
With your help, they can reach the most vulnerable people with food, clean water, medicine, shelter and much more when they need it most.

Disclaimer: the author has no relation to the UN and donating to the NGO is just suggesting that a donation be made to the NGO but it is not a **requirement.**